LIKE WE STILL SPEAK

**ETEL ADNAN
POETRY SERIES**

Edited by
Hayan Charara and Fady Joudah

Like We Still Speak

DANIELLE BADRA

The University of Arkansas Press
Fayetteville
2021

ISBN: 978-1-68226-176-7
eISBN: 978-1-61075-751-5

Manufactured in the United States of America

25 24 23 22 21   5 4 3 2 1

Designed by Liz Lester

⊖ The paper used in this publication meets the minimum requirements of
the American National Standard for Permanence of Paper for Printed Library
Materials Z39.48-1984.

Library of Congress Cataloging-in-Publication Data

Names: Badra, Danielle, author.
Title: Like we still speak / Danielle Badra.
Description: Fayetteville: The University of Arkansas Press, 2021. |
    Series: Etel Adnan poetry series | Summary: "Winner of the 2021 Etel
    Adnan Poetry Prize, Danielle Badra's Like We Still Speak addresses
    notions of inheritance, witnessing, and intimacy in a world on fire"—
    Provided by publisher.
Identifiers: LCCN 2021003578 (print) | LCCN 2021003579 (ebook) |
    ISBN 9781682261767 (paperback) | ISBN 9781610757515 (ebook)
Subjects: LCGFT: Poetry.
Classification: LCC PS3602.A365 L55 2021 (print) | LCC PS3602.A365
    (ebook) | DDC 811/.6—dc23
LC record available at https://lccn.loc.gov/2021003578
LC ebook record available at https://lccn.loc.gov/2021003579

Supported in part by the King Fahd Center for Middle East Studies
at the University of Arkansas.

For Dad and Rachal,
until we speak again.

CONTENTS

III.

SERIES EDITORS' PREFACE

Like We Still Speak gives both physical and metaphysical form to grief. The physical form comes from the poet's need to control and negotiate loss, but not necessarily because she is in denial or distant from acceptance. Rather, in Danielle Badra's hands, form becomes the body with which she upholds her life against the fear of disintegration and forgetfulness. In the process, she finds herself ecstatically smashed with the pleasure of survival, a palpable thrill that affords her the force to forge and sing her remembrance, her elisions, her eucharist. Even the title of the book transfers the untranscribed into the translated. How much of our speech is still? What begins as an elegy for her sister expands into an elegy that includes her father. What begins as a careful construction of effigy becomes a pliable imagination of commemoration—accuracy gives way to fracture; perfection is scattered into fragments; preservation gives way to multiple voices and echoes.

The more Badra toils with form (compositionally, structurally, linguistically), the more the metaphysical emanates from the page. This is a deeply spiritual book, all the more so because of its clarity and humility. Yet, we cannot walk away from the addictive command that so many of these poems ask us to follow: to read them along plural paths whose order changes while their immeasurable spirit remains unbound. Each poem is a singular vessel—of narratives, embodiments that correspond with memories, memories that recollect passion. The columns in many of the poems here are contrapuntal but are also echoes of the hemistiches of the classical Arabic qassidah, and of the well-preserved ancient ruins of the soul.

Like We Still Speak is structured like a rosary strung together with several different types of recurring beads. Take, for example, the "Station" poems (there are four in all), or the pair of "Counting Down" poems ("Slowly Counting Down from Ten" and "Slowly Counting Down from Ten While Taking Deep Breaths"), or, among our favorites, "Ode to Onion" and "Ode to Honey." With any rosary, however, the beads are more than ornamental, and they also serve a purpose much larger than that of marker or placeholder for this prayer or that breath. They initiate a practice: an experiential practice that leads, ideally, to solace, reflection, or even epiphany. In this way, *Like We Still Speak* is a sanctum. Inside it, we are enthralled by beauty, consoled by light, sustained by making.

Fady Joudah & Hayan Charara

I.

(Sister)   *(Sister)*

sitting on
sandy beach
toes dipped over
freshwater's cold edge

sandal lines seen
on her so tan feet
sunning herself asleep

                                        she carries her
                                        poems like figs

                                  shaken from the tree
                              of knowledge or heartbreak

                                  or picked from a window
                                          in Lebanon

                                                calling them figs
                                        does not describe her harvest

                                                or her for that matter
                                                    it does not tell you

                                            how important she is to me
                                            or everything i haven't said

she is still on the beach
she is always

up shore from me
almost close enough to witness her
barefoot markings falter mid-sand

i will follow her faded trail
she is still astray
from safety & from land

into water
it starts waist deep and drops
off quick she holds
her breath

i am worried for us
the hourglass is stagnant
is sideways

i can't recall
our childhood
all on my own i can't
remember when

we became sisters
embracing in mom's blue robe
or when she first held up my head

sometimes i worry
that the next time we meet

we will no longer know
each other she

will dream in idioms
that i don't understand

or she will not
understand why my fire

has never
burned as fiercely as hers

                                        there is always the hope
                                          that we can hold out

                                        our harvest to each other
                                          we will see and savor

                                        everything we need to
                                        though this would mean

                                              that i would have
                                             to pluck more than

                                                        one fig
                                                        a year

photographs are not sufficient
to tell her story

i know she loved me eventually
but love was after worry that
i'd be better loved than her

snapshot of two kids
piled up on a paisley couch
with mom euphoric

there are parts of her
that i will never know

or if i did know
they would not mean
what they should

she has outlived
what i wish i could
take away from her

what hurts most
was left unresolved

there will always be
this fig

sitting in my
stomach rot

undissolving
she is not to blame

i am not to blame
too

if she can read this
she is haunting my hands

trying to talk
or type in Times to what
she was i am

sorry if i'm wrong
it's been so long since we last laughed together
was it February

when we
facetimed four years ago

it was
her smile that made me cry

                                        i would
                            if that wouldn't take away
                                        her fire

                            which is something
                                i could never do

i only hope that her harvest
            will not become like

                            dead birds
                            swollen

                            with guilt
                    and decomposition

i hope that it will remain
like figs to her
nourishing if small

and beautiful despite
the heat of the sun
i hope that she will grow

like the fig trees
that live in her

through cracks
in the earth's rind

i sobbed over
the color green this morning

olive bikini
at the bottom of her plastic tub

of summer clothes
that looked better on her
than me

she always knew how to
dress me

how to braid my
hair like i braid

her words
like we still speak

Inheritance

That feeling   that mutilated apple now mush beneath my boot
that pervades   coats the orchard ground in an aroma of utter decay
all my being—   that saccharine soil mother carried a daughter across.

On edge, jumpy,   the feeling I get now when I get too close to rot.
Vigilant, on patrol—   the putrid stench of autumn prepping for tundra
while on the outside   my body resists a glimpse of death's willing gaze.

I try to look   at my body in the full face of the new moon
composed, in control,   the smile I make for good measure
laid-back even.   The smile of a triggered pain.

What a fucking   saccharine fruit? What willing gaze? This
tightrope   is a fresh-squeezed lemon smile. I intend
to walk,   to stay like this for a long while.

Station

unaffected lately
      daylight lingers before full morning
            in the dull space between

            two slices of slightly buttered oatmeal bread
      two eggs over easy-medium
feed the one with the broken yoke to the lucky dog

start the car defroster and pray
      the way leads neither east nor west
            into the foggy air of freezing cold

            reverse down the driveway
      once the rear windshield melts enough
to see clearly the slick road

arrive at work early
      park in the empty lot
            walk to the office with a forest view

            two brown squirrels chase tails up tall oak trees
      stare off into half-sleep
wake startled by snow falling from gutters

go home and let the lucky dog sit at your side
      read "whispers in the loggia"
            before the stations of the cross

take the lucky dog for a long trail walk

watch a Tigers baseball game

text the youngest daughter

why can't my religion be soft and easy?

eat a few thick slices of pink lady apple

brush the sharp skin from between back molars

wash away weighted sighs under the heaviest shower setting

lock the lucky dog in the laundry room and head to bed

remember the eldest daughter who died eight years ago

dream of her

Sister, I've missed you. I relinquish your yellowed skin. Or death. Sleepless, terrified I'm next in line. Writing bullshit emotions, lamenting about PTSD, about dead ends. To collapse, my my my. I can't control. I can't risk the same but quiet, sobered up. Russian roulette red. Nail polished toes. French manicured fingers flinch.

Sawing myself in half. Spent days leaving my body where not even I could find it. I have nights lately looking for my body because thoughts would be useless without hands, and lips I would not enfold hips, touch, whether fever or chill or if a mouth could stop me from unnecessary words forming.

On a sticky barstool. A twenty percent tip. Counting down. Waiting for answers or swollen from standing so long. A full disclosure. Restless legs on melatonin. A new heart with measured beats. Panic attacks are as divisive as forced similes. The postapocalyptic drought. The freshly mopped floor buckled at times like broken ribs. Your face was after crashing. High as fuck. Crashing still. Unmuffled silence. Hard footfalls. Counting down a deep breath.

The Short Way   &   *The Long Way*

She died   Her father awaited
within a week.   her last breath
Over her bed   from across the glass
in the ICU we prayed.   as tubes were removed
We sang the body plastic.   kidneys donated too.

We who loved her,
we watched her tremble,
we dabbed her dry mouth.

                                He recited *The Prophet.*
                                He would never mourn
                                like everyone else
                                bearing dogwood trees
                                weeping her name,
                                        Rachal.
                                He heard
                                her sweet voice in a deep sleep,
                                breathe it in—

We waited
for her eyes
to open again.

For her to see us   *every day—*
holding her,

saying, *it's ok.*   *that death will be a warm reunion,*
                                whenever he's ready.

There is a storm coming. The thickly painted clouds will press their way in. Your house, sunlit in its glossy

flowers will fade, if not fall away entirely. There will be only grey left. Grey scooped out with a trowel, pasted on.

there was a grey painting on display that day a traveling exhibit she was told to rotate through monitor the artwork make sure it isn't touched tell everyone to just breathe it in she worked her whole life for this moment the chance to stand and study light the way it forms pigment on canvas a white wall in an old windowless

room she prayed for this perspective her heart pasted on with a trowel she always knew there was a storm coming one she had met before been soaked by such torrential she walked around prepared for it pen ready and paper she sheltered her words close she must have known this would be her final Rothko her last time worshipping in the stark open chapel a poem in the black book she kept in her purse she carried it with her while she worked the collection guarding art and guiding art lovers where the greens and reds of the flowers will fade sunlight is carefully located the thickly painted clouds will press their way in will rearrange the way she lived so close to vibrant colors her arm hair electric her skin aglow in a way she understood the aftereffect of living and how it pays homage to both birth and death all in one fleeting moment she predicted that there will be no room for light in halls

You will breathe it in. It will fall on your children as you kiss them goodnight. They will carry it with them.

whites and blues will be blotted out, darkened. There will be no room for light in your halls. The greens and reds of the

Pianissimo

Hands inclined
ascending along lines where
notes fall inside a sanctuary.

Love
a nervous staccato
nearing atonement.

Leaning away
from an epic étude
she improvised cacophony
escaping into decrescendo.

Her ear
an effortless tempo
solely her own.

Her illness was graceful
as Rutter's Requiem
yet she offered no harmony.

Gazing at the Unforgettable: Baba's Fragments

Well, hello. I never know what I'm going to know next. Unscrew my hands and wash them. Ergo sum qui sum. There's too much history here. You know, of course, that you are the epitome. I'm glad that you were born the way you were and that you were born. This is the part in the movie where we cry. There are times that touch. This is one of those times. Eventually, we'll get the wallpaper. I'm gonna miss this place. When I first came, I learned church. Command me, command me. I was crying last night. All of this had to mean something. I know exactly how I'm going to sleep tonight. The first thing I do when I wake up is go back to sleep because I don't want to wake up. I don't want to get rid of you. Goodnight sweet princess. Bricks and stones may break but when it's warmer I will walk you around the villa. When I walked into the earliest place, well, I thought, "Do we know what we know." I don't know why but I love you. I don't know what to say when I pray. Spread yourself a thousand ways. Take me with you.

It Is

I have been told,	"love cannot alter it."	I did not need to be told.
A eulogy ends at the funeral.	Words cannot add to it.	Like everything else.
An elegy tries too hard.	You yourself have survived it.	Like nothing else.
Ash is not only dust, but bits of bone	& so,	like everything else
that once was draped in marigold,	you must carry it.	Like everything else,
a dress rests in my closet,	a thing that carries itself	I have been told.

Elegy for the Eldest Daughter

Always, Mom's kitchen window latched shut above the sink.
On the ledge just outside sheltering wisps of snow, my mind
frozen solid or a slow drip. Forever the Christmas pine is

nearly naked from frequent ice storms. In sharp wind
off Lake Michigan limbs lash against the fence line, my heart,
a twisted metal boundary defining the backyard. Cardinal

where we worked ash through calloused hands into topsoil.
Wooden box filled with bone fragments left open, the window,
latched shut beside a garden where we planted blue lilies.

When the moon was full and the sun stayed up past ten, blinking
stars settled in the bark stripped branches before flickering out as fireflies
across a frog pond that was once filled in with fat koi fish: black, white,

bright orange. Your life— a grey heron stealing breakfast before full morning,
now, a graceful felon inflicting loss. Roost of red-crested birds disturbed
along the laundry line, cardinal wings cut across the blinding white.

2.14.12

I was just waking up

she pulled away

a wrecked sleep

EMTs said

a blanket and gown

concealed her convulsing

on Valentine's Day

where bandages crossed

her open heart

that day

crossed over

became a dream

was a wakeless

sternum

cardinals awaiting

cadaver

around ribcage below

tubes of blood

that kept her

breasts

rising

which lay unharmed

10. Sister, sawing myself in half on a sticky barstool, I've missed. Spent days, a twenty percent tip, you leaving, counting down.

9. I relinquish my body waiting for answers or your yellowed skin. Where not even I, swollen from standing so long, or death could find it. A full disclosure.

8. Sleepless, I have restless legs, terrified nights lately on melatonin.

7. I'm next looking for a new heart. In line, my body with measured beats.

6. Writing bullshit because panic attacks. Emotions, thoughts are equally as divisive. Lamenting would be useless as forced similes about PTSD without the post.

5. About dead hands, apocalyptic ends, and lips drought.

4. To collapse, I would not enfold the freshly mopped floor. My my my hips buckled at times. I can't control touch. Like broken ribs.

3. I can't risk whether your face was the same but quiet fever or chill after crashing, sobered up, or if high as fuck, crashing still.

2. Russian roulette red, a mouth, unmuffled silence. Nail polished toes could stop me from hard footfalls.

1. French manicure. Unnecessary words. Counting down. Fingers flinch forming a deep breath.

Mama's Waltz

mama as child was loved
less than bottles of gin
watched her world
waltz off tempo
while her mama
imbibed she hid
no one seeking her

mama cuddled me
clinging to her
leg like a merry-go-round
ride I learned
how to hold
happiness like a
happenstance

An Entire Universe

| I thought of | your voice |
| how | I listened to it lilt |

| at that moment | I lost an entire universe |

| I realized | worlds crumble |
| I was | without oxygen |

| crying | into scattered asteroid belts |
| while | comets burn on impact |

| | I am somehow |
| smiling | still alive |

Station

Grandmother helped me realize we are meant to be carriers of light, not bearers of darkness. Who mourned Lebanon and innocence the smell of thyme and sesame slow roasting in the oven. The smile on my face before communion wafers and wine reminiscent of her last supper in Upper Galilee where figs were sticky when ripe and fish was blackened on both sides and she ate the eyes first. She sold her gold wedding ring to pay back debtors during the Great Depression. Grandfather laid car parts for Oldsmobile in Lansing to feed his family. He dreamed of Greater Syria and the streets of Aleppo where he gave milk to strangers under full moonlight.

Permanently

A storm is coming	fleeting across fields of color
thickly painted clouds	pipe smoke out an open window
press	black ink into a bowl of reduced-fat milk
your house	a canvas
sunlit in glossy whites	greens & tangerines
& blues blotted out	torn apart
no room for	your accident
light in your halls	altered to look like art
greens & reds of	rust-colored hinges
flowers fade	ochre & orange & red on red
fall away	
entirely	gathered in the garage beside
only grey	your favorite painting
left	folded up
pasted on	a faint aroma

you will breathe it in

Mother Once Told

head of black curls,

once told me

we are like the rhododendron,

which blooms large, bright, and

heavy in the woods,

belonging

to the far place where

the sun rises, even if

everyone has forgotten

whose shoulders are load bearing,

once told me

struggle is a noun we carry with us

in pockets of shadow

where light never pauses.

I watched my sister die

beneath the moon's still shining,

her shoulders still.

I held her up.

Ode to Onion

Onion is the only thing I want to eat.

My great uncle ate raw onion dipped in sugar for lunch.

When my tears are meant for my ancestors,

I'm more Lebanese than Michigander.

My tears taste like red onion saltwater.

I lick them from my hands, a favorite meal.

A meal I've shared with my sister before in a pillow fort.

She cooked more often than me.

I always did the dishes in the evening once the sun set.

It is easier to focus on the moon crest out the kitchen window.

I prefer the light of the moon to other forms of far light.

If light must be distant let it be moonlight.

Flashlights in the coat closet.

Shadow puppets across a backlit wall.

We were static after rubbing ears with withering minks.

We were learning to curate our own culture.

Father

Faithful apple
taster

relishes the core.

A poison
at the center.

Every variety
he's eaten

in pleasure. Sinister

Eden lodged
between his teeth,

his narrative
includes

hunger

an embellished
eternity

his hallowed

ulcers

enshrine.

Sister

Sarcastic
idol
singer

tempting
even
rational

minds to adore death,
inciting envy
from the very angle

of radiance.
The ground paces
near her image

as though endemic.
As though her
only sorrow is

resilience,
not necrosis.
Her own

nebulous
magic. Her empire,
tragically

crimson, lilts.

How to Read to Your Father in His Hospital Bed during a Global Pandemic

Use the speakerphone setting and place the phone a short distance from your tired mouth.
This is the fifth call you've made to your father who forgets when it's morning or evening.
Tell him again that it is Good Friday and let him respond, "Oh good."
Your father, who left the priesthood for parenthood, returned to bless pews every April.
Tell him, "It was once our destiny to walk in the garden." Await his response, "Dani Baby."
Forget the words that no longer hold meaning and focus instead on the ones that do.

    I.   "Why can't my religion be soft and easy?"

    II.   "How many times am I supposed to lose my loved ones?"

    III.   "We expect each other never to fall."

    IV.   "You will taste the salt of your own tears."

    V.   "We're talking about loneliness here."

    VI.   "Let's stay hurtable rather than hard."

    VII.   "I carry your image within and without me."

    VIII.   "The negatives can have meanings too."

    IX.   "Help us learn all over again how to love enough."

    X.   "Teach me to simplify my life."

    XI.   "What a death it must have been."

    XII.   "In the shattering silence—be still."

    XIII.   "Holding your bruised body in my arms, I feel a weight lifted from me."

    XIV.   "All creation held its breath in the deathly quiet of that tomb."

Listen to your father repeat between each station, "We touch the wood of your cross
and we remember." And we remember.

Slowly Counting Down from Ten While Taking Deep Breaths

sister   sawing myself in half   on a sticky barstool
i've missed   spent days   a twenty percent tip
you   leaving   counting down

i relinquish   my body   waiting for answers or
your yellowed skin where not even i   swollen from standing so long
or death   could find it   a full disclosure

sleepless   i have   restless legs
terrified   nights lately   on melatonin

i'm next   looking for   a new heart
in line   my body   with measured beats

writing bullshit because   panic attacks
emotions   thoughts   are as divisive
lamenting   would be useless   as forced similes

about PTSD   without   the post
about dead   hands   apocalyptic
ends   and lips   drought

to collapse   i would not enfold   the freshly mopped floor
my my my   hips   buckled at times
i can't control   touch   like broken ribs

i can't risk   whether   your face was
the same but quiet fever or chill   after crashing
sobered up   or if   high as fuck crashing still

russian roulette red
nail polished toes

a mouth
could stop me from

unmuffled silence
hard footfalls

french manicured
fingers flinch

unnecessary words
forming

counting down
a deep breath

II.

Child of the Universe

I can't dry your tears.
I can't find your mother in the crystal rubble.

I can't cradle her cracked skull.
I can't shield your doe eyes from shrapnel.

I can't soothe your skin from white phosphorous blooms.
I can't keep you as my own.

I can't make you leave Aleppo.
I can't smuggle you out of scorched streets.

I can't teach you the constellations through smoke plumes.
I can't reveal your fate at the bottom of a broken teacup.

I can't control your seasoned screams
or even fetch a pail of water.

I can't sing you a lullaby to the unsteady beat of barrel bombs.
I can't tell you to close your eyes as I can't close mine either.

I can't bake baklewa for you without orange blossom water and walnuts.
I can't cook rice for you without controlled flames.

Or give you sweets without bees without flowers without hives.
Pour milk without an udder a breast or formula.

I can't promise you will survive to write poems and not be bitter.
I can't paint a peaceful scene for you if war never ends.

I can't stop the sky falling.
I can't stop the rain stinging your open wounds.

I can't dull the blinding sun
or kill for you.

I can't comb your dusty hair.
Tie your tattered shoes.

Replace the love that once held you.
Collage your face into a portrait.

I can't face your infinite stare.
I can't hand you some sugar, some rocks.

This distance is not light-years but oceans and yet
I can't reach you this year or the next.

Fire

give me an ancient song
and I'll give you a forbidden light

syllables that slide from front teeth

as backdrop for gods to grow colors
from pinpricks into calligraphic prints
                                    of my mother
she is not the sun
she is what comes after: you

are made in her image
are dancing in her clothes

my wild hair
in the spring wind glows

I carve shadows at the ground
beneath your feet

Lunacy

I will not be
your masterpiece—

I do not revere
the art of subjugation

you want me framed
on your wall

The artist paints
to glorify himself

But I do not revere
your self-obsession

I cannot sit still
for portraits

a crazy woman—
whatever that means.

lunacy
in full moonlight:

my brain and belly
dance in separate directions.

around an abandoned bonfire
composed of canonical books.

gold leaf paper flames swirl
up in a gust of cold air.

I melt slowly
like soft leather bindings.

America

that

in the eyes of my country

I am one of those people

who have darkened and dirtied

America

that to at least

one man

I am a threat

I wonder if

he knows

night

I was waiting with bottle rockets

with illegal Indiana fireworks

with bang snaps and sparkler swords

I was waiting for the new moon

an empty cicada shell

unlit lightning bugs

I ignite the summer sky

when hot air hits heavy breath

I'm beautiful and dangerous

Self-Portrait as Pandemic

I dance in a museum empty of relics.

An illusion of my calm is a mirage and it makes us less alarmed to catastrophe.

We never panic on Saturdays.

We let laughter alter requiem and rewind the underlying mania of us.

Errands in the yard.

Up with the sun.

We return to mourn in the evening as an offering to night.

Station

when Aunt Mary was born her mother
| loathed her for having Father's face
| | loathed Jido for forcing Mother's hand in
| | | holy matrimony before age eighteen
| | | | Father found Mother stuffing grape leaves
| | | | | Mother never wanted his weighty fingers
| | | | | | folding her family's food the wrong way
| | | | | | | eating the excess rice & raw meat
    I   too   am   marked   for   ever   I
| | | | | | | |onions dipped in sugar|
    carry   your   image   within   and   without   me
| | | | | | | Father got what he desired every time
| | | | | | Father had what Mother deserved too
| | | | | whatever Mother longed for was forbidden
| | | | whatever Mother lauded she lost at conception
| | | when the highest form of luxury was love
| | something Mother knew nothing good about
| a man with an insatiable taste for olives
a woman with scarred olive branch arms

Ode to Honey

Honey ends up in my hair even after I've licked my fingers clean.

Peanut butter and honey sandwiches were all that I would eat in elementary school.

My first day of kindergarten I was stung by a bee on my hand after eating a PB&H.

For robbing its hive and leaving remnants of mischief on my small palms.

Red-handed and throbbing I entered my first day of school tearful and full of guilt.

I crushed and killed it as it stung me for stealing from its glistening hive.

My fingers curved inward toward the middle of my palm as a reflex as a defense.

The stinger was stuck when I first raised my hand for permission to be excused.

The school nurse had a comfortable cot I escaped to when I was feeling overly stimulated.

After a certain age I didn't speak much about what happened to my swollen hive.

Not even my sister knew until I was seventeen and invited to take back the night.

We sat side by side on a stage at Bronson Park where we used to take field trips.

We found burial mounds there and shared our family's secret.

Our family secret is orange blossom scented, sticky, bitter and it stings in the palm.

The Calypso Deep

I.

Rubber rescue boat
leaking gasoline onto
battle-tested feet.

II.

Soon we will catch fish
whose flesh was fed
by our own.

III.

Do we all drown now
in the way of unity?

IV.

A pomegranate branch,
as makeshift life jacket
across the lap of a child
who did not choose this life.

V.

The life that did not keep her
and the life that did.

On Passing

I passed as white?   : olive skin tanning easily in the sun
as normal as safe   : hairy forearms and fuzzy upper lip

as sure of who I was   : a woman with imperfections and allure
until America's past   : bushy eyebrows bridging big brown eyes

caught up with me   : plucked and waxed and cut
and held me down   : scarred kneecaps from childhood scrapes

and told me this is   : a wound that never fully heals
who you cannot be   : high cheek bones and bulbous nose

I passed by becoming   : bitter and educated and quiet
insubstantial   : heavy bangs hung from a furrowed forehead

substance does not change   : a life rife with questions unanswered
without fire   : glittery red nail polish on pedicured toes

without blood   : pierced ears and Arabic script on the right hip
without pain   : whiplashed long neck and spinal scoliosis

without losing   : a heartbeat with erratic rhythm
where I began   : sister with Sito's hard stare

This Is Why I Can't Be Your Lover

You want me to forget the face of death
so that my smile will be beautiful again.

The word beautiful isn't around anymore.
And I am only impossible.

If you thought it was that easy to forget
the way death trembled at the bombing

of booksellers, of Baghdad and bindings.
When an idea was beautiful and dangerous,

begging for safety. Or my father's prayers
for his daughter's pained face just before

they shut down her breathing apparatus.
I watched his eyes form the doomed edge

of whatever he was of a cloud's downpour
before catching her last gasp of air.

I can't smile and recall that beautiful end.

Embodiment

All tongue   this language of disorient,
               this transliteration of lipstick is wicked   and wet.

All hungry,   all delineated darkness in absence of light,
               or presence of red, abundance of liquor in my   haunted throat.

Today,   corporeal, is controversial, is intentional,

                                                   what we do,

is secret: the lost breath between shots.

Origins

From

guns	crucifixes
fall mornings	olive oil
damp leaves	grape leaves
skunk piss	basement arak

to cover   to burn
it all   it all
up.   up.

From

land	famine
not my own	not my own
all mine	all mine

we worked it   we breathed it in
with our own   with our own
hands. For generations   orange blossoms. Forever

we have come from kitchens—   we have come from fauna—
three square meals, the garden,   figs for breakfast, thyme for lunch,
before this—no decay.   without this—no breath.

From

dirt	sea
gravel	salt
dusty fingernails	safe harbors

backwards and backwoods   hilltops in Tibnine
dead apples   dead pomegranates
and arrowheads.   and crusader castles.

For generations we came from   For sanctuary we came from
these woods—these hallows now   those streets—those holy now

                              hollow.

Molten

Raw heat of my childhood,
brotherhood with a boy blew into my veins.

Those stories, those pomegranates' pierced seeds,
sour juices oozing through bruised rind—shred the boils

off this skin, hollow this honeycombed cavern.
Lava coursing my capillaries, love ephemeral as a brother

who let loose his curio by pummeling my arteries,
hide or seek in his back shed, shocking my heart into seeing

that same hatred holding my OshKosh overalls
at my Achilles' tremble.

I Was Told to Break the Cycle

and it was violence beckoning violence to come back again

stuck in an ache for more ache and aching for someone to suffer

like meat ground up in a meat grinder still needs more grinding

in our teeth the gristle of muscles we wanted to forget

the fear we feared for repetition of the same sad mistakes

in our throats an obvious scream for someone like me to echo

we refused the refuse of our inheritance of a pain passed down

to go on this way to go on this way to go on this way

Ghazal for Lost Women

Under the harvest moon there is always a camel & the camel is always a far lost woman,
lost to the world she once inhabited of red wine and unleavened wafers. Woman

wafting scent of orange blossom seeping from attar syrup cooled on the kitchen counter,
counter to the culture of her mother who baked with anise seeds instead of walnuts. She

walled herself inside her fearful heritage when the once world's center certainly collapsed,
collapsing her English into Arabic attempts for fresh watermelon, bateekh woman.

Bateekh, her favorite word to pronounce when she was unfamiliar with phlegmy letters.
Let her return to the camel & the camel return to her a sense of discomfort like the day she

hid beneath pines playing with the boy next door a game that made her feel monstrous.
The monsters under her mattress were really inside her all along, terrorist woman,

terrorized by the thought of an evil side to her bloodline, of suicide bombers and martyrs,
martyrdom was never all that appealing in comparison to mediocrity, the average woman.

Rage is relative to bloody knuckles and what it was they were fighting for. For her huriya,
freedom is relative to the laws that bind, she was bound only to her body, scarred woman.

Scarab beetles stood for reincarnation in Ancient Egypt, said to push across the sky the sun.
Deadly woman, *deep is your longing for the land of memories, dwelling place of desires*, al-shams.

III.

Arabic

I am not
writing a poem
about you

that is not   the oud
what this   is
is   extraordinary

I am only   every other syllable
putting down thoughts strummed
on paper

thoughts
about you
yes

but   *ukhtee*
only   I will memorize
thoughts—   the language of my dead

they are not
so permanent
as a poem yet

they are   rising from quieted earth
only words   a desire to summon *mindoun*

Happiness Often Lasts When My Love Is Yours

Apple-picking
in the fall
as originally
our presence
was tense
and sweet
and verdant
under the pressure
of an eclipse.

Our trees
were everbearing
and intensely red
despite the nature
of such saccharine
nectar. We enacted
salvation.

Water

If you can remember the prayer
I'll listen for your praise

refill your fire-felled forests
flourish your scorched fields

if it isn't too late for faith to work
to wash my face in blue gold

draped in lapis lazuli my silver hair
still trails from my fastened chariot

four white clouds are empty overhead

maybe your wisdom was wrong
when you erased my elegy

the dark grey of rain
the hard sting of sleet

on unexpectant skin
on the earth as she cooled off

to replenish me once more.

Station

I see you Father raising your body
by your own spirit in a family picture
at Kom Ombo your sacred daughters
and carved crocodile reliefs honor
Sobek who protected Middle Egypt ages ago

kept home along the crooked Nile
ibis roosted among papyrus reeds
long like cattails to camouflage river
monsters in muddy sand and alabaster
columns temple walls worn away

in flash floods and sandstorms but
never completely collapsed when you
fell ill your heart stopped flowing for a few seconds
before being reborn unlike your eldest daughter
who continually died until she didn't anymore

immortal handful of her flesh
incineration blemished by fragments of pinkish brown
bone puncturing the plastic bag she sleeps
inside a sarcophagus of sand and cedar
inlaid with mother-of-pearl

the board you used to play backgammon games on
painted lapis lazuli sky with naked Nuut's night
extended below the price in Egyptian pounds
for a photograph with your family

The Thick Bark of Someone Who Is Hollowed

Now that　　　　　　　　　I am older
I understand　　　　　　　Death—
what it is.　　　　　　　　I was young

to feel　　　　　　　　　　when I first met you—
that smack of wind.　　　　Your haggard hands shaking
against bark—　　　　　　　my scarred wrist.

I cannot,　　　　　　　　　you missed my hand,
blame you　　　　　　　　　by an inch.
I, too,　　　　　　　　　　with wounds

have wanted　　　　　　　　my heart
to be unmade,　　　　　　　beat faster,
to be pulled back　　　　　　to heal unveiled veins.

Relieved　　　　　　　　　　you knew
the burden.　　　　　　　　One difficult thing,
of being alive—　　　　　　　Death.

To carve out　　　　　　　　my labyrinth,
the wood at her center　　　　would not end
and live there　　　　　　　　that day

like an animal.

Arboreal

Maple
baked onto
rusted ecology.

An allegory
for what's lost
before it becomes extinct.

Opulent pollution
the stars are keen
to shine but
linger in smog.

Lichen-infused
earth offers
temporary lungs.

Every temptation
exists to die.

Only gardens dwell
on the glory of years
spent resting and yearning.

The Garden of My Agony

Always. Always say always.
   Only today can we say our story.
A thousand small Persian horses sleeping
   safely.

   Yes, the syllable sprains like a dry branch
in the plaza with the moon on your forehead.
   Come out and shine like a crocus shines
when I embrace your waist four nights.

No one knows the perfume
   that ignites our alphabet.
No one knows the martyrdom
   half lost in a pollen dusted lawn.

   Do not question elegance. The world opens up to you
between gypsum and jasmine.
   Do not ask the word what shapes each side.
Your body is a fugitive of always.

Enemy of the snow
   stamped on a worn wall.
A hummingbird of love between the teeth.
   This is not what we are; nor what we want.

Tributary

Stars cannot be seen

        tattooed on your sandal-settled feet

in the Tiber at night

        swinging in a spring swept breeze

swallowed by

        the river's balancing bridge

the mouths

        hands holding tight to statues

which lie

        to the left and to the right

at the bottom

        imagine letting go

sleep

        sinking into silt

in darkness

Some Days Honey, Some Days Onion

staggering is grief my days some
song wild a was who sister my
and silence dead a her after
out held notes piano like sound almost echoes
laughter cavernous her of echoes
whole was once heart my where ribs my across ring
before was I who of half am I

plural the not ة singular the

alone while even dances still 1
hips my move can I music without even
living for rhythm balanced a find can I
death from away move I house haunted a in
altars across scattered artifacts her
Rome from candles artisan unlit
days some dust gather

يوم عسل ,يوم بصل

Yeheya's Portrait of a Poet

The charcoal lines of her wide hips hiking
up to meet my blackened fingertips; at a distance
I was certain she would sit with me, and watch
my sketchbook fill with dim figures
as sunset gave way to dusk and stars.

The sand beneath our feet was still and still
it spread inside hollows of my paper's
heavy tooth; texture held her blurry frame
as she inhaled my hand-rolled hash and exhaled
the Milky Way; *her reason and her judgment*
wage war against passion and appetite.

        My hand held on to her
words, incessantly inserting letters—
where her hair should be an Arabic ح
wraps around her square ث face and س breasts
her long ا legs; her body belongs
to calligraphy; lingering silence
between each mid-August meteoroid
alight on earth's cold edge of endless space.

I handed her my cigarette before
she took it to her sunburned lips, and let
the smoke return to her a sense of sin;
the desert inside her.

This Is Just to Say

I have taken the   time to memorize your
heart—aorta, left   right to open and close any
ventricle—   unlocked doors, rusty hinges,
you kept chilled   hidden; a peeling coat of red paint
in your ribcage   screws are starting to fall out,

which   I was not anticipating.

You were   an empty frame
probably saving   a warm welcome
for someone who,   walking through holes in walls,
deserved it.   Behind crumbling brick—

forgive me,   a calcified façade—
it was so beautiful,   obscenely unseen
as it thumped   inside your house,
its last beat in my hand,   a fist-sized mound of flesh.

A Candle from Rome, Italy (2003)

the reason why I never lit the wick before now
pollinated pistil of a tiger lily thick with wax
petals of bright orange & burnt yellow & almost alive eleven years ago

on the way to the Pantheon I purchased a candle
at an artisan's stand in an ancient square called Campo de' Fiori
where Giordano Bruno burned at the stake for watching the stars
& acting out the art of memory

my father stared there at the bronze statue & wept without words
my sister & I watched my father weep at the feet of an old martyr
my father would not weep like that again

until he held my sister's hands while she was seizing
I watched him weeping while my sister was seizing
we held hands

Love Poem

We eat orchid for breakfast.
This love is an outlier.

Interpreter of my sighs, you ask
What is it?

When I bought the print of two women,
I didn't yet know it would be of *us.*

My heart,
trouble builds above our valley.

Beloved, your neck is soft and sweet
in the morning.

The image is usually of rock,
I see a feather—

your willingness to be
blown in the wind of my grief.

My mouth moves *anger,*
but means to say *gratitude.*
You cannot, will not.

Luminous point, incandescent,
a star is both light and bomb.

Love Poem

A rosemary olive oil toast.
This loaf is still soft at the center.

One or two slices, habibti?
You say you see mold on the crust.

You say throw the whole thing away.
I cut the crust off and feed us anyway.

Pumpkin buttered in late autumn.
We survive on the slight rot of winter.

You, who display gerbera daisies
at my bedside, in an old saké glass,

balanced on the brink of catastrophe.
You are graceful with your loss,

your fruit cored. I am
always decomposing.

Your mouth moves *night,*
but means to say *luminous.*
I have to relive that lunar cycle.

You and I are moonshine.
The stuff gold is made of.

"(Sister) (Sister)" is a response to a poem titled "(Sister)" that my sister wrote for my twenty-third birthday. I didn't recognize the weight of this gift until after she died.

"Inheritance" and "Mama's Waltz" include portions of writing from my mother's notebook.

The "Station" poems are in response to my father. The stations refer to the stations of the cross Catholic mass he delivered every Good Friday. "How to Read to Your Father in His Hospital Bed during a Global Pandemic" incorporates lines from his stations mass.

"Slowly Taking Deep Breaths," "Slowly Counting Down from Ten," and "Slowly Counting Down from Ten While Taking Deep Breaths" incorporate lines from my sister's poem "Magician."

"The Phillips Collection" is framed by my sister's final poem, which she wrote on Valentine's Day 2012 while working at the Phillips Collection. "Permanently" is in dialogue with that same final poem.

"Gazing at the Unforgettable: Baba's Fragments" is made up entirely of words my father spoke over the last month of his life.

"It Is" incorporates fragments from Anne Carson's *Nox*.

"Elegy for the Eldest Daughter" incorporates a Facebook post my mother made on my sister's Facebook wall after she passed. It read, "Always on my mind. Forever in my heart. Cardinal out the window. Wondering what would be in your life now. Love you."

"2.14.12" incorporates a line from Corinne Schneider's poem "Talking to Rachal."

"An Entire Universe," "Lunacy," "America," "The Thick Bark of Someone Who Is Hollowed," "Tributary," and "This Is Just to Say" include my sister's poetry in the left-hand column and my response in the right-hand column. Rachal's poetry is almost exactly the same as it appeared originally, with minor adjustments to the capitalization and punctuation.

"Mother Once Told" is in response to E. Rhödes Huyett's poem "The Labyrinth."

"Child of the Universe" is an ekphrastic poem in response to artist Mojdeh Rezaeipour's *Child of the Universe* (2016).

"Fire" and "Water" are ekphrastic poems in response to work by artist Nahid Navab.

"On Passing" is in dialogue with my sister's poem "On Passing." My sister's poem is in the left column.

"This Is Why I Can't Be Your Lover" is in conversation with Diane Seuss's poem "I'm Glorious in My Destruction like an Atomic Bomb."

"Embodiment" is an ekphrastic poem in response to artist Jessica Kallista's *Shift Freedom* and in conversation with her poem "Sulca in Subspace."

"Origins" is a poem in dialogue with Melanie Tague's "Origins in Two Parts." Tague's poem is in the left-side column.

"Molten" incorporates a line from Meg Chuhran's "Molten."

"I Was Told to Break the Cycle" incorporates a line from Aaron Coleman's "Viciousness in Ends."

"Ghazal for Lost Women" and "Yeheya's Portrait of a Poet" incorporate text from Khalil Gibran's *The Prophet*.

"Arabic" is in dialogue with a poem by my sister. The Arabic words used in this poem are *ukhtee* (my sister) and *mindoun* (without).

"The Garden of My Agony" is a mash-up of two translations. The first translation is from the work of Federico García Lorca. The second translation is from the work of Eugenio Montale.

"Some Days Honey, Some Days Onion" is in the Arabic form, created by Marwa Helal. The Arabic form is to be read from right to left.

"Love Poem Love Poem" is in response to and in collaboration with Holly Mason's "Love Poem."

ACKNOWLEDGMENTS

For my sister, Rachal, whose life ended abruptly and way too early, whose language will forever inform mine, and whose love I will always mourn.

For my baba, who challenged my understanding of being human, who loved laughter, and who left me gazing at the unforgettable.

For my mama, whose strength and warmth in the face of disaster is inimitable and whose bear hugs can cure any ailment.

For my love, whose ear for poetry is impeccable, whose heart is poetry too, and in whose arms I will always dance.

For all my loved ones, my sibling-friends, my poet friends, thank you for your support and love through seemingly endless grief.

To Corinne Schneider, Diane Seuss, Meg Chuhran, Mojdeh Rezaeipour, Nahid Navab, E. Rhödes Huyett, Jessica Kallista, Aaron Coleman, Holly Mason, and Melanie Tague—all collaborators on and contributors to this manuscript—thank you for being open to dialogue and for sharing your voice in this conversation. To all those who submitted work to the original thesis project this manuscript came out of, thank you for entrusting me with your creative energy.

To my professors and mentors—Diane Seuss, Gail Griffin, Sherry Ransford-Ramsdell, Sally Keith, Susan Tichy, Peter Streckfus-Green, Jennifer Atkinson, Eric Pankey, Amal Amireh, Zeina Hashem Beck, Philip Metres, and Brian Teare—thank you for your close reading, support, and friendship.

To Hayan Charara and Fady Joudah, thank you for opening my eyes to the parts of this manuscript that I did not see and for helping to form it into a thing that carries itself.

Thank you to the following journals that previously published versions of the poems in this manuscript: *Outlook Springs*: "Permanently," "The Garden of My Agony," and "Slowly Counting Down from Ten While Taking Deep Breaths"; *45th Parallel*: "Arabic"; *The California Journal of Poetics*: "Ghazal for Lost Women" and "This Is Why I Can't Be Your Lover"; *The Greensboro Review*: "Embodiment"; *Bad Pony*: "Station" (originally published as "The Sixth Station"); *Rabbit Catastrophe*: "Molten"; *Duende*: "Mother Once Told" and "Love Poem Love Poem"; *Beltway Poetry Quarterly*: "Elegy for the Eldest Daughter," "Station" (originally published as "The Eighth Station"), and "Inheritance"; *Mizna*: "Some Days Honey, Some Days Onion"; *Cincinnati Review*: "It Is"; and *Guesthouse*: "(Sister) (Sister)."

Thank you to Finishing Line Press for publishing my chapbook, *Dialogue with the Dead* (2015), where the following poems first appeared: "Tributary," "An Entire Universe," "Lunacy," "America," "This Is Just to Say," and "The Thick Bark of Someone Who Is Hollowed."